Bloodlines

It is as if, to remain genuine, Gypsies must live only in gutters or in poetry.

— Alaina Lemon, *Between Two Fires: Gypsy Performance and Romani Memory from Pushkin to Postsocialism*

for Violet

Bloodlines

Sarah Wimbush

Winner of the
Mslexia Poetry Pamphlet
Competition

SEREN

Seren is the book imprint of
Poetry Wales Press Ltd.
Suite 6, 4 Derwen Road, Bridgend, Wales, CF31 1LH

www.serenbooks.com
facebook.com/SerenBooks
twitter@SerenBooks

The right of Sarah Wimbush to be identified as
the author of this work has been asserted in accordance
with the Copyright, Designs and Patents Act, 1988.

ISBN: 978-1-78172-594-8

A CIP record for this title is available from the British Library.

The publisher acknowledges the financial assistance
of the Books Council of Wales.

Cover artwork: Rebecca Morris
www.scrappingontheedge.blogspot.com

Printed in Bembo by 4Edge Ltd, Hockley

Contents

Bloodlines

In the Bloodlines
there's a hooped earring.
In the Bloodlines there's an open vardo
door, ramsons on the other side. Songs and seasons
wave at you from the Bloodlines, atchin tans watch you
fly. In the Bloodlines there's an acorn of swagger that
inflates into a barrel wearing a vest. In the Bloodlines
there is nothing to offer up to the Old World except
a pair of shammy bootees –
your past, their past.
Bloodlines stare,
bemused by the
chant of Tables,
a company car;
lunch. Bloodlines
hoick slingshots at
woodcock and snipe.
Damp earth is a must
as you lie with the Bloodlines,
some scratch the name of the wind into elm with a crotchet hook,
others chor lollipops from children. Bloodlines can't hear you but
they follow you in a handful of photographs and crumpled vowels:
the shortening clay pipe; *gorgio fowki*. In the Bloodlines you make
yourself make steamed pudding, then eat salad. In the Bloodlines
there's a long blue thread. In the lea and the lanes there must be
someone who can tell you about the Bloodlines; about
the rhythm of your tongue, your flying fox glare,
the need to set curtains ajar at night.
What are you searching for
in the darkness? Why are you?
And yet, it's the Bloodlines
that murmur on the barval,
Bloodlines that understand
the spell of a campfire,
your attraction to gold,
how if I shuck my paleface
from gullet to hairline,
the world would turn
scarlet and all that pours
out will be road.

atchin tans stopping places;   *chor* take/steal;
gorgio fowki non-Gypsy/Traveller folk;   *barval* wind

Weaving with Rushes

This is the walking gal weaving rush by the marsh
with the end wound over, and then laced across.
Fingers that nip cats' tails and twist harvest dolls,
fingers that knead bulrush stems into blackberry bowls.
How she digs for her roots with a reed-mace rod,
spinning wands into webs as the vardo moves on.

Watch her pour mutton fat into earthenware jars,
turning pipes to rushlights inside molten lard,
and fills chair bottoms at the next butter cross
and schtums flattie-jib and in her wisdom walks on.
Is this her face on the riverbed telling our story,
are these her footprints stomped in the bog behind me?

Defy the gorgios with their gyppos' cries,
meet me in the shallows, our silhouettes entwined,
where we shall wade out together fishing for reeds,
all those fragments and threads raddled inside the weave.
With the end wound over, and then laced across,
this is the walking gal weaving rush by the marsh.

gorgio non-Gypsy/Traveller

Carroty Kate

I am dressed in last night's campfire
and dead men's boots.
My hair is the colour of a thousand foxy hawkweeds
and I own one red skirt
and a navvy's tongue.

I get by dukkering at the next market place
with sheeps' trotters
or a brass groat as payment for the reading,
my kissi belt strapped tight
to my left thigh. Time was,

you would have slapped me in irons,
dragged me to York Tyburn in a hay cart sat on my coffin,
where I'd be dropped
from the Three-legged Mare —
just for being.

dukkering fortune-telling;   *kissi* purse

Pitched early mornin' at encampment o' Gypsy king Esau Smith

Not the circuit of wheat-lined drums
between Lincoln, Doncaster and Hoyland,
but Black Patch, its slag heaps rolling out
before their wooden wheels like a sea of tar.
That place, Smethwick, was said to be
on the other side of the Black Country,
but Lizzie would say: *so weir did't blackness begin,*
n end, fo this is't blackist country as eva known.
Already the vardo's fruit carvings would be bruised
with dustings of pitted charcoal; the piebald, Plunk,
draped in a sooty horse rug; the little ones
playing with kin on the cinder mounds,
faces polished as any darky folk.
On his return, her man was bear-black –
from the peak of his trilby to the toes
in the holes of his boots – a hard day
carting furnace waste from Soho Foundry.
While Lizzie scoured the slack with her sisters,
Hannah and Cinderella, digging for treasure
through the scoriae; metallic gems, glass-chinks,
glossy vonga, the shushi poaching all afternoon,
the sun doused to the arc in a farrier's horseshoe.
And magic blossomed, like naphtha lamps
held high over the forges and smelt works –
time to eat by the yog, share the old songs –
smoke Black Twist in clay pipes, liquorish ribbons
spiralling into throat-tightening bitterness,
the darkness beyond littered with diamonds.

vonga coal;   *shushi* rabbit;   *yog* fire

Gal

I pause by the yog's blooming furze,
twilight unfolding its flittermouse wing
till I close like a hand into a fist.
Tethered to the seasons –
winter's gub on my skin, our jib in my song,
the drums roll skywest beneath my heels.

Here, I take only what I need
from the borrowed earth, hold gorgios
in my needle's eye, ask no favours.
And yet, in times of want there is nothing
I will not steal, nothing I would not give
to kin or the hedge-mumper or the manless.

Woman to the master of the grai; mistress
of sheaves and the flame-eyed hare,
I tame my smoldering curls and my otter bite,
press on with the doors, yearning
for the atchin tans where trees nurse the sun,
the places with whispered names:
Hagg Lane, Misson Springs. The Garden.

gub curse; *jib* language; *drum* road; *gorgio* non-Gypsy/Traveller;
hedge-mumper tramp; *grai* horse; *atchin tans* stopping places

11

John Thomas

He is the chav of the mam, drowned in a river accident
like a paper boat on her maiden voyage. He is the son
of the fatha who lost the plot, brought to roam wi nowt
but a hip-flask n compass in his hedge-mumper pocket.

He has a grandmammy who can skin a cat wi one shpeal
of her tongue n wastes two penn'orth on his gooin school.
Sixteen and he's pushin Grandma in her wicker bath-chair
up Huntingdon town n back, then stands with his chap

in his hand n his back to the wall wi the girl next dooar.
And his fingers gets trapped in the housemaid's drawers.
And he does a bunk to Godmanchester hiring fair.
And he's with Lord George Sanger's Circus fouar year.

He's wi lass after lass posterint next town. He's the rum'un
wi two lassies ont go, hoistint Big Top n tekin it darhn.
He's on the reigns cartint bear cage to Attercliffe: nods off,
rolls off, watches the steel-rimmed wheels trim his loaf.

He's an odd-job man, a pot man, a fish man in Tickhill village.
He's at the Gypsy encampment; he's the talk o the pitch,
the flattie whose heart beats a rhythm for Lizzie, his lass.
He is a rag man, a scrap man, a ganger, a this-n-that man.

He's a div wi that fat gal overt chip shop in Worksop.
He's a good fo nowt old bloke arght on his ear int doghouse.
He's a returner, a sometimes earner, loves a beer,
a bet, his chavs, his wife. Loves flyin his kite.

A Sund'y in Worksop

That morning, we pitch our caravans on Joe White's,
somewhere on Sime Street. Mother scrubs vardo floors
with washday waste, singing *Paddy McGinty's Goat* or maybe

I'll Take You Home Again, Kathleen. Daddy has a bloke to see
at The Old Ship Inn or perhaps The Robin Hood, God's people
blinking as they enter daylight. I stay with the tub cart

or was it the dray, water Plunk our dapple pony, or was it Spike
or was it Pluck? A school of men march into the yard, keen to win
a fortune with Pitch and Toss. From a corner the look-out boy

watches me. Beneath the sign, 'No Gambling Or Spitting',
the chuckers bless a fat penny each and bowl against the wall,
or could it have been into the air? Metals wield and thud.

Hoots and oaths. The men drift away, one lad left on the floor
or maybe leant against the wall, says over, *fot in't war, I did –*
and he has no hat. Or was it boots? Or was it both?

I can see Sandbeck Hall

and lady housekeeper standing at the servants' entrance
and the onion sacks filled with steel pans, rabbit skins, cast-offs,
and the two wide skirts belonging old Lady Scarbrough.

And Daddy doffs his trilby, grease stains around the rim,
like a posh mush in his best gorgio: *thank you dear Madam.*
And when it rains it rains and we sit it out beneath the dray,

and after several days the rags are dry, and the two wide skirts
go to Black Jess, the Maltby washer lass. And Daddy makes a bob.
And Jess swaps her old fella's hobnail boots for an orange.

mush man; *gorgio* non-Gypsy/Traveller

Breakfast

The caravan nods
the tilly lamp pendulum –
a Traveller rhythm.

Now and then lodger
Noah, rises from the floor.
Slips away. Returns

with ten partridge eggs
in his trilby: stokes the stove.
Tapped. Split. Blubber spits.

Stripped from knife to plate.
Shared between eight. Each bite fresh
as today's sunrise.

Threshin'

On stubbled dust, field-workers gather
by newfangled machines; firebox stoked,
boiler banging hot to blanch and bubble

a clutch of corncrake eggs gleaned by Sam –
still warm from their bed of hay, chopped
on rough-grained bread and shared.

The lads hayfork stooks onto the stage
to feed the spinning drum, where it is said,
men have been dragged and eaten

up to their waists. Here, my sister Liza
(the day's band cutter on a man's wage)
cuts the twine and downs the sheaves

while our smallest take root on banks
with grandmothers, twisting gold into hats
and hearts and corn dollies. At one point

the thresher is stalled, to unpick a worm
of binder twine burrowed inside the straw.
Stoppage: uses light, loses brass –

but spoiled bedding can fell a beast if eaten.
I'm to keep the chaff hole clear where bract
is winnowed off the ears, and whooped

from the machine; chaff dust, hellish stuff –
bristles inside my headscarf, my shirt,
those moist places. Under florid skies

with florid faces, us girls splash
into Scrooby pools, scrub with willow sprays,
then head back, arm in arm, to our pitch

inside a bender night; to rest on a log,
to share a scrag of ham and tatts.
The earth still warm as the air turns cold.

bender tent

Meat Puddin'

Take shin, kidney, an onion. Dice.
Cradle beef suet in your palm; shred
into flour with Daddy's rabbit knife
lace-edged with rust. Add spring water.
Pullt goo into a ball.

Roll into a circle with a besom end.
Scoop the mas and press onto the dough.
Gather like a pack-up. Flute the rim
with a lick of ale to seal together.
Gi the dumplin' skin a slap.

Turn onto a floured pudding cloth.
Tie a double knot. Slide into the cauldron,
water thrilling over scavenged vonga,
one eye on the blip–blip–shudder till dusk.
Lift puddin' arht b't knot. Untie.

Ease the moon into an Imari bowl
haggled to a farthing from Black's pot barrow
on Retford market. Cut into a clock.
Add cooking liquor and salt –
n' then lass, eat wi carrots, tatties, swede.

mas meat; *vonga* coal

The Bittern

After the glut of soft fruits,
and oat cakes toasting on the griddle,
and the deluge of Cox's,

it's the wintering-over
in two-up two-down cottage,
vardos stored on Big Frank's piece,

a squall of pheasant and quail
bartered for a tail-end of hogget,
mother schooling us by the range:

how to baste the skin to gold,
how to skim the fat for rushlights
and axels, how to eke the meat out

from pink to grey to dry; scraps
for soups, bones coddled to slate
in washday broth. All cushti scran.

And the hardness of spring.
Bitterns nesting in reed beds,
sweeter than heron –

the male's deep *whoohu-whoohu*
like a breath blown over a bottle.
On a still day, I feel that call for miles.

cushti scran good food

Grai

How the mare watches you
watching without blinking,

the shire horse dragging her away
like a bundle of rags.

How the knackers placed the muzzle
behind the dark pool of her eye

a new thought blown
across her vision. The simplicity

of soil and water
and man   splitting her shank

after three lads… no four
forged a pig's squeal from a piebald.

And the shouting   the shouting
as they had tossed the rope's hoopla

over the royal sweep of her neck –
the peculiarity of those whinnies

the light's attention
drawn to her dragon breath.

At a time of no shadows,
tufts of grass

down at the hawthorn's groin
where the field unearthed a bog.

grai horse

Our Jud

Sometimes he dug the ditches out on Serlby Hall Estate.
And thrashed his sister's man after he'd slapped her 'cross the face.
And often carried water for his mother from the Ouse.
And thieved ten shilling Great War pension off his brother Hugh.
And sang like an angel and played grass like a tin whistle.
And rarely missed a fisticuffing down the Old Blue Bell.
And that time calmed the lady's filly bolting up the road.
And couldn't write his name but nose-to-tailed a bookies' board.
And got away with it that night those skewbalds went amiss.
And took a fair old beating 'cause he loved the married lass.
And didn't give a monkey's or ailed one day in his life.
And always wanted chavvies but never fancied a wife.
First to rise for threshing, last in a cock-fighting wager,
the man named after kings and coins and a dragon slayer.

chavvies children

The Calling Basket

Black velvet trim for mourning mantles are long-tails.
Mother-of-pearl buttons are a pair of lost souls.
Tapes, bindings and cord are pegs honed from hazel rods
sewn into the pleats and seams of ladies' bodices.
Elastics are willow girders for pants and drawers.
Nottingham lace is the pacing green at Thorne horse fair.
Threads are exotic birds from the Indian subcontinent
or a front parlour in Rossington. Broderie anglaise
is filigree cast in a foundry. This Old Holborn tin
is a bow-top wagon: acorn thimbles, ratter's teeth clasps,
press-snap hail; hooks and eyelets are twigs and leaves.
Needles are hobnails. Cotton reels are vardo wheels.
Ribbons are smoke signals for missies' pigtails and china throats.
Centuries on the doors as queens of the Underworld.
Centuries walking the lanes as dust: a cup of tea in the desert,
read the leaves. The kindness of last year's bib and tuck –
thank ya kindly lady, yous be lucky. And gorgios
who hide behind lock and book and jacquard curtain –
this young monisher who buys a bud of lace,
her rush to cross my palm with brass.

long-tail rat; *gorgio* non-Gypsy/Traveller; *monisher* woman

The Hedgehog's Tale

She said a true Gypsy
wears an earth-brown neckerchief
dotted with box patterns, so fine
it flows like air
through his wedding ring.

She said, a slope near a river
is the best place to find a spring;
dig a hole,
watch the sand settle –
careful as you fill the kettle.

She said, you can feel rain coming
by the weight of the wind
and good scran
is as close
as a hedgerow and a fine tree –

spikes wrapped in clay and baked
in a firepit, sweet
as a chestnut
then ripped
to suck the pith and juice and squeak.

Mother Tongue

i

Dukker is to see
the future, or your fortune,
while *dik* (sounds like deek)

is the word for look
which in my Yorkshire lingo
would be 'gis a dek'.

Eye translates as *yok*,
while *yog* is fire – and a branch
is firewood or *kosh*.

ii

The voice a wild *grai*
(rhymes with eye) – a lexicon
of *jib* in my mind

wandering the land
over centuries, arrived
flaming, restless, thinned –

word legerdemain,
those Anglo-Romani psalms:
'*cushti*'... '*trushni*'... '*tan*'.

grai horse;   *trushni* basket;   *tan* place

iii

King Esau stories
'gutter Gypsy poetry' –
a fine *mush* who'd *chor*

the earth to protect
the poorest - their Robin Hood.
Some said deviant

others said brother
(pal from the Romanes *phral*)
I say: our Father.

iv

And the *Rom* renowned
for his *Jowi Grey* – as far
north as the Blacklands

where coal is *vonga*
(can also be money) – or
Brit. crib: 'wonga'.

Gorgio means neither
deep ravine nor incessant
hunger. However....

mush man;   *chor* take/steal;   *Rom* Gypsy man;
Jowi Grey bacon and potato stew;
gorgio non-Gypsy/Traveller

Late Afternoon by a Hedge

You insist on removing the black apron,
comb your fingers through those tangled curls.
I can see you pulling on your crocheted top,
the one it took two summers to make.
Your checked skirt seams are perfect. The mud
brushed away from your dancing shoes.

Hannah's arms hang from her shoulders
like dead rabbits, her face numb with fatigue.
But yours, yours tilts in defiance –
even when standing still you're moving.
You stare into the camera's blackness,
our eyes meet. Behind you there's a barn,

familiar, but then, I can't be quite sure.
The grass is long. Perhaps it's harvest time.
You buy a print from the travelling photographer.
Hannah sits by the campfire. You wrap
the crocheted top around the photograph.
Place it in your corner inside the vardo drawer.

Lizzie

Pale-ale baby. Afeared a nowt.
The earth at her feet
from Hawks Nest to Tangye.
Wickem gal: untrammelled,
scene-shifting from daffie time
to the last golden acorn.

Thread-fiddler. Drum queen.
Wide-winged in those in-between places.
Speaks the language of twigs and brocks and sheaves.
Stripper of alums and beets –
fallers and walnuts sacked-up
for the Christmas calling.

Her nose-warmer a faithful companion.
Her snow-white nets drifting
across June beech. Babes as tall as trees.
She is Smithereens in some distant plot,
her headstone a touchstone,
her heart grassy-green.

drum road;   *nose-warmer* pipe

The Ring

Imagine. Her hands snatching necks.
Shushi skins pinned into borrowed earth.
How she scrubs the gubbins from her garnet setting,
flogs the pelts to furriers for a bob or two.
That lift of soft fruit between her finger and thumb.
Peas. Beans. How she buffs the harnesses in readiness
for Thorne Horse Fair – the Romani and Irish on the flash,
the open-lots and Burtons in a horseshoe around a yog –
fiddlers, jigs on boards, the clack-clack of spoons,
Jowi Grey on the wind, then spudding at Serlby.

Watch her travel through fields, lanes, cobbled brooks:
posting rag-bills, hawking daffodils,
how she grips her lad's hand as they do a runner
to wed at Tinsley Church. And always that sense
of moving as one. The sky a hard master –
drums snug as an owd pair o chokkas,
carting castings at Steel Peech and Tozer
to Tickhill encampment hawking pots
to the hubbub of Black Patch mid-winter,
to those wide flat hayfields around Misson Springs.

How sometimes she only knows slack and air
and her wits – the atchin tans: Foundry Lane,
Great North Road, Gibbet Hill, Attercliffe.
No half-dead frills only her histories
and the seasons: the earlies, the hoe, wheat stooks,
mother's calling basket, wintering-over,
rabbit skins parched to stiff tambours.
Imagine this ring – my grandmother's ring.
Its Gypsy setting. Its golden eye burnished
with all the jib and ancients it has worn thin.
See, here on my finger. How it fits.

shushi rabbit;   *Gypsy setting* similar to a bevel setting;   *yog* fire;
Jowi Grey bacon and potato stew;   *chokkas* boots/shoes;
atchin tans stopping places

In the Library

I stop-start on my journey along the multi-coloured shelves,
pull out three books. The black and white man

pushes past; his arms swish-swishing like swords,
his palms damp with newspaper print.

My granddaughter and I sit at the reading table.
We have lived through every circle in the English oak.

I read to her from the Bible, and then *To Kill A Mockingbird*.
The black and white man blows his nose. Everyone looks up.

He marches past us: bigger, fatter. Blacker. Whiter.
Something flutters from his pocket to the floor.

My granddaughter runs across, picks up his library card,
holds it out to him. He takes it with a smile.

Back on my lap her blonde hair is rue and woodsmoke.
I open *We Are The Romani People* and read to her.

Acknowledgements

Acknowledgements are due to the editors of the following publications where some of these poems first appeared: *Brittle Star, The High Window, The Interpreter's House, Mslexia, Stand, Strix.*

These poems, or earlier versions of them, placed in the following competitions: *Pitched early mornin' at encampment o' Gypsy king Esau Smith* received third prize in the Black Country Museum Poetry Prize 2016; *Threshin'* was commended in the Binsted Poetry Competition 2017; *Carroty Kate* was shortlisted in the Keats-Shelley Prize 2018; *The Bittern* was highly commended in the Rialto Nature and Place Competition 2018; *The Ring* was a runner-up in the Mslexia & PBS Poetry Competition 2019; *Weaving with Rushes* was longlisted in the Alpine Fellowship Prize 2019; *Bloodlines* received second prize in the Ledbury Poetry Competition 2019.

I am grateful for all the help and encouragement I have received on my poetry journey: to Jane Draycott and David Morley and the Arvon Lumb Bank group May 2019; to everyone at New Writing North and my amazing co-New North Poets: Freya Jackson, Penny Newell and Charlotte Wetton; to my dear writing pals Jayne Shipley and Heather Clark; to *Mslexia*, Cove Park, Amy Wack and *Seren*; to artist Rebecca Morris, and to my Claire and Jess, and Rob.

Special thanks to all the incredible poets at York Stanza for their friendship and support over the years, with particular thanks to Carole Bromley and Stuart Pickford without whom these poems would never have been written.